TURTLES AND SNAILS

by Gallimard Jeunesse
and Gilbert Houbre
Illustrated by Gilbert Houbre

A FIRST DISCOVERY BOOK

SCHOLASTIC INC.

New York   Toronto   London   Auckland   Sydney

Turtles and other animals with shells live all over the world.

One of the largest turtles is the giant tortoise.
One can weigh as much as three people!

Most turtles that live on land
are called tortoises.

Freshwater turtles

Red-eared slider

European pond turtle

Spiny turtle

▲ Red-eared
slider head

▲ Softshell turtle head

▲ Snapping
turtle head

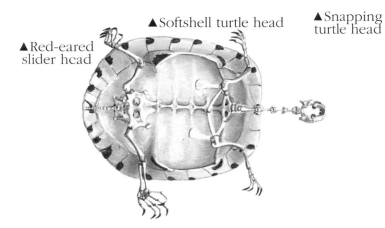

A turtle's shell is part
of its skeleton and cannot
be separated.

Shells help protect turtles from harm.
Most turtles pull their head, feet, and tail
into their shell when they sense danger.

Primitive turtles pull their head in
sideways. More advanced turtles can pull
their head straight into their shells.

Land turtles eat plants. Freshwater turtles
eat plants and small animals. Sea turtles eat
crabs, turtle grass, sponges, and jellyfish.

Some turtles live in marshy areas…

European pond turtle

…others live on land.

Spurred
tortoise

Desert
tortoise

Box turtle

Hinge-back tortoise

These turtles live in salty water...

Diamondback terrapin

Hawksbill turtle

...and these live in freshwater.

Softshell turtle

Matamata

These are freshwater turtles...

Big-headed
turtle

Spiny
softshell turtle

Green turtle

...and these are sea turtles.
Freshwater turtles have webbed
toes, which help them swim.
Sea turtles have flippers.

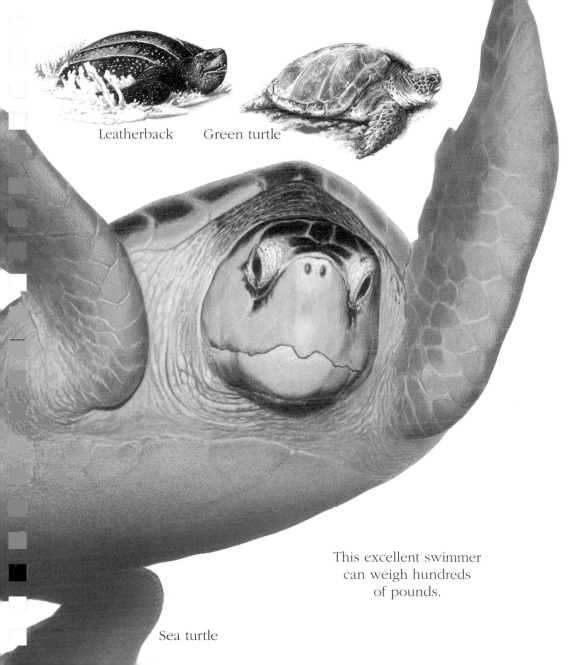

Leatherback   Green turtle

This excellent swimmer
can weigh hundreds
of pounds.

Sea turtle

In the spring, turtles mate.
Several weeks later, the female digs
a hole in the ground and lays her
eggs. Then she covers them up and
leaves them to hatch. Sunshine
keeps the eggs warm.

Turtles hatch out of their eggshells when they are ready to be born. That can be from several months to more than a year after the mother leaves.

The newborn turtles scramble up through the dirt to the surface.

What animal lives
in these beautiful shells?

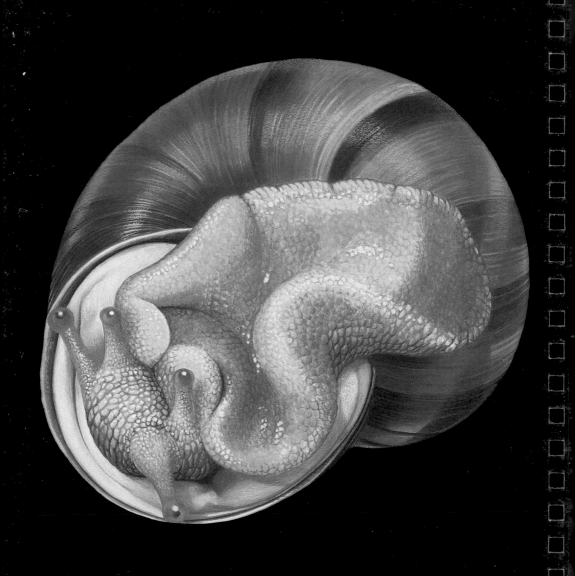

A snail!

A snail has feelers called tentacles.
Its tiny eyes are behind the tentacles.
It pulls itself
along on a smooth
muscular foot.

These snails live on land...

Striped snail

Forest snail

Snail of Burgundy
region in France

...and others live in the water.

Sea snail

Periwinkle

Tree snail

Giant African
land snail

Ramshorn
snail

Freshwater snail

Lymnaea snail

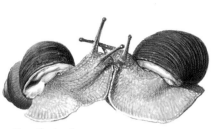

Snails belong to the mollusk family of animals, creatures with soft bodies and hard shells.

When spring comes, land snails lay their small eggs in damp hiding places, such as under fallen leaves.

A snail's body is soft and flexible. It can climb up trees and over almost anything that gets in its way.

Land snails are herbivores, which means they eat plants.

Snails have teeth. They chew pieces of plants in their small mouths.

Land snails produce slippery mucus, which helps them glide.

When winter comes, land snails find a cozy spot among the fallen leaves. Over the next few months, they rarely come out of their shells.

But in the spring, the snails
venture out again, ready
to enjoy the warmth and fresh
food that the season brings.

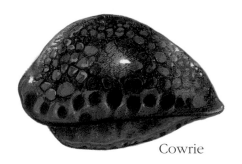

Cowrie

Here are some other animals
that live in their own shells.

Barnacles

Bubble snail

Lima or
File scallop

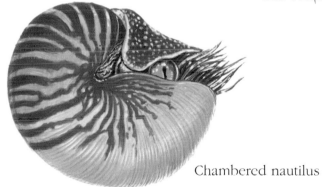

Chambered nautilus

Certain animals, such as
the hermit crab, don't have shells of
their own. They live in the abandoned
shells of mollusks.

Armadillo,
walking

Armadillo,
rolled into a ball

These animals don't have shells, but they have
tough outer layers that are as strong as shells.
Don't they look interesting?

A mother and
young armadillo
are covered with
bony plates.

A tree-climbing pangolin has large horny scales.

The porcupine is protected by sharp quills.

Library of Congress Cataloging-in-Publication Data available.

Originally published in France under the title *La tortue: coquilles et carapaces* by Editions Gallimard Jeunesse.

No part of this publication may be reproduced, or stored in a retrieval system, or transmitted in any form or by any means, electronic, mechanical, photocopying, recording, or otherwise, without written permission of the publisher. For information regarding permission, write to Scholastic Inc., Attention: Permissions Department, 555 Broadway, New York, NY 10012.

ISBN 0-590-11764-5

Copyright © 1991 by Editions Gallimard Jeunesse.
This edition English translation by Wendy Barish. Copyright © 1998 by Scholastic Inc.
This edition American text by Wendy Barish. Copyright © 1998 by Scholastic Inc.
This edition Expert Readers: (turtles) Dr. Michael Klemens, The Wildlife Conservation Society/Bronx Zoo, and (snails) Dr. Paula Mikkelsen, American Museum of Natural History.

All rights reserved. First published in the U.S.A. in 1998 by Scholastic Inc. by arrangement with Editions Gallimard Jeunesse, 5 rue Sébastien-Bottin, F-75007, Paris, France.
SCHOLASTIC and A FIRST DISCOVERY BOOK and associated logos are trademarks and/or registered trademarks of Scholastic Inc.

10 9 8 7 6 5 4 3 2   8 9/9 0/0 01 02 03

Printed in Italy by Editoriale Libraria
First Scholastic printing, August 1998